THE OFFICIAL

JUSTIN BIEBER

2017 Annual

centum

Hi there Beliebers!

WOW! What an amazing year it's been and it's all thanks to you! It's because of you I'm living the dream! You've been with me all the way and I'm so lucky that I get to spend my time doing what I love most – writing and making music for you, all my wonderful fans. I love you guys! Every one of you is special to me. I wake up every day knowing I have the best fans in the world. My team is my family and you all deserve your time to shine too.

I've packed this annual with loads of posters, fun facts, puzzles and activities about me, my music and performances. I hope you enjoy. Don't forget to tweet me @justinbieber and #GetCloser with me @Bkstg and @shots. For all my latest news you can check out my website www.justinbiebermusic.com too.

Love yourself!
Justin xxxxxx

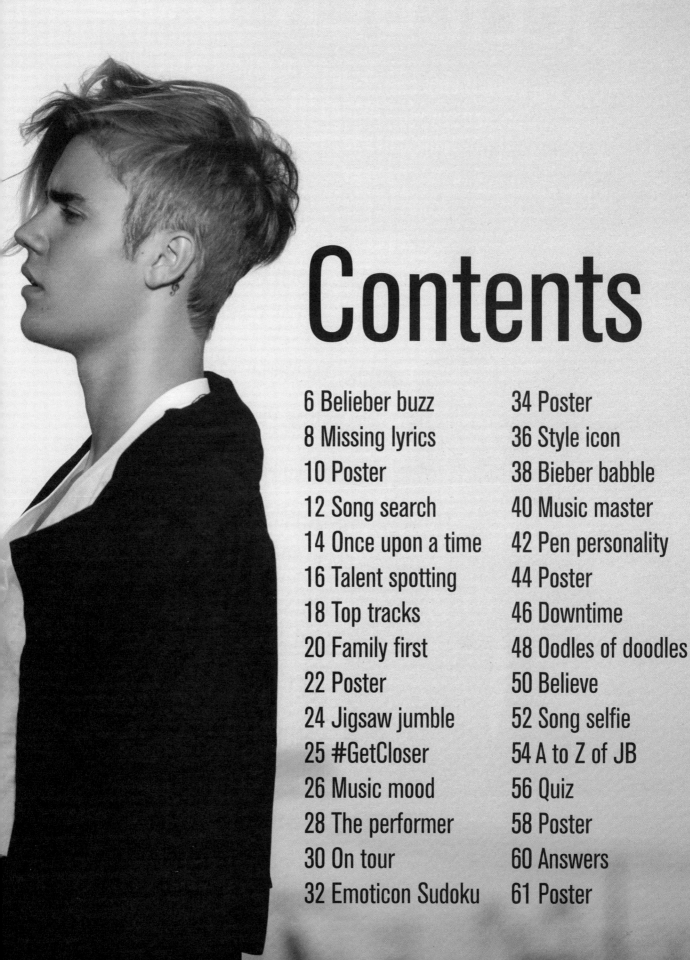

Contents

BELIEBER BUZZ

Think you know Bieber? Think again! This book is the ultimate fan guide, packed with fascinating facts and truly random stats. By the end of this book you'll know every single thing there is to know about Justin, but for now... let's start with the Bieber basics!

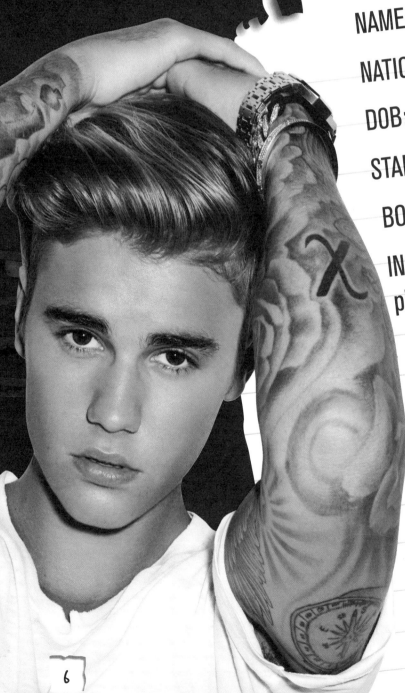

NAME: Justin Drew Bieber

NATIONALITY: Canadian

DOB: 1st March 1994

STARSIGN: Pisces

BORN: London, Ontario, Canada

INSTRUMENTS PLAYED: drums, guitar, piano and trumpet

LOVES: basketball, ice hockey, Italian food, funny YouTube vids and his FANS!

PET: Esther, the cutest pooch ever!

MOST LIKELY TO: release hit after hit after hit...

STUDIO ALBUMS RELEASED: 4 so f

TWITTER MENTIONS: around 60 a second! #GetCloser

100% SUPERSTAR

10% fashion follower

5% family

10% Italian food

15% sports fanatic

5% funny

5% generous

50% singing sensation

7

MISSING LYRICS

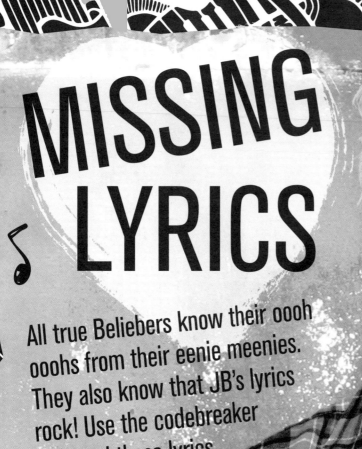

All true Beliebers know their oooh ooohs from their eenie meenies. They also know that JB's lyrics rock! Use the codebreaker to reveal these lyrics.

LOVE YOURSELF

A N D I F Y O U

A B C D E F G H I J K L M N O P Q R S T U V W X Y Z

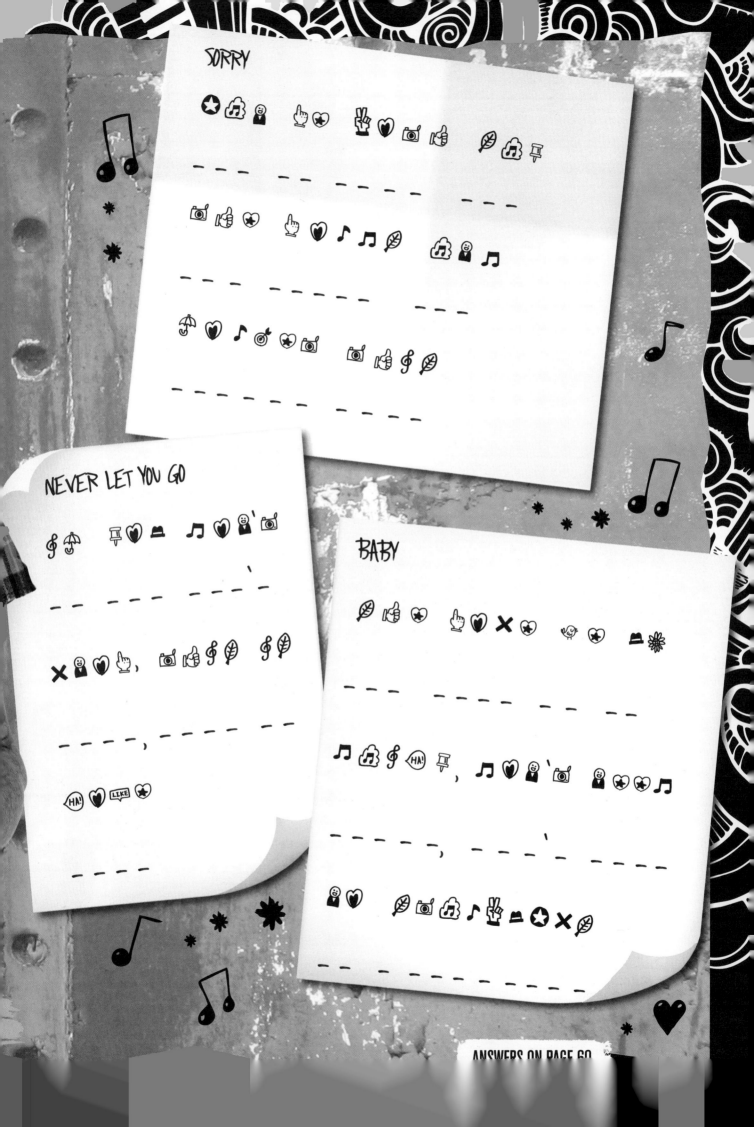

SONG SEARCH

Get into the Belieber zone by finding all of these amazing hits in the grid opposite.

- Baby
- Boyfriend
- Confident
- Down to Earth
- First Dance
- Hold Tight
- Heartbreaker
- Love Yourself
- Pray
- Sorry

```
R B J F X R S U H J E M J L I A F E F V
V M X H B K V U B L C O O H V K Z Z F Y
W K V J T J A U H C W O Z Q K C V K K Z
J B D Y F M A H R C E D N A E K W N F A
A F U R G K V C E D N M S V C E J M P D
L K W O W M U I O W Y N E G C E J E N P
N H P Z L B U P Y Y R I C E J K A O R S
D E Y L M Q S R E E R C A C I E K C R H
M A E C N E L E T Y F F Y I F E K A R F
A R V I K S M I W Q Z F E C T I G H N F
N T R L U E H Z B W H O L D T G H N P
P B F F O R U N B K Z B S J E F O N P
C R L J B G V V A A P H E Z B I E C R P
K E Z H P X W B X Y I M O D N B Q J T N
M A I M Z V M B X G E X I D P G Q T J
G K T G Z M S T K K G F S F Z G K Y S I N
F E W X M L G T Z A O B M O D M S T J
O R K F I M U X Z I U O L G R D G E W G
Q L A D H Z B I L C B J B P R Q G S W H
D P I X J B Q E E G S E T B R W Z G P Y R
I A U N E Z L A M W S X T A D A H N Q X
H T R A E O T N W O D Y W Z U M Y R J X
```

HOW DID YOU DO?

LESS THAN 5 MINS
BELIEBER BRILLIANT!

LESS THAN 10 MINS
JUST-IN TIME!

MISSING A FEW?
KEEP ON BELIEBING!

ONCE UPON A TIME

...not so long ago, a boy called Justin was born and raised in Canada. He went to school, hung out with his pals and dreamed of becoming a star. Lucky for us, he followed that dream!

SCHOOL RULES

Justin's first school was Jeanne Sauve Catholic School. He loved music and sports lessons the most and it was here he met his bests buds, Chaz Somers and Ryan Butler, who are still his friends today.

HOME SWEET HOME

Justin grew up in Stratford in Ontario, Canada. Like many who lived there, Justin learned to speak French as well as English. Bonjour Bieber!

Population: 30,000

MISCHIEF MAKER

Teachers remember JB as a leader. If he behaved the whole class behaved, but if he got into mischief, then so did everyone else! When his music career took off, Justin left school to be home schooled, which he loved, as he only had to do three hours of lessons a day.

CHILD STAR

Justin began to experiment on the piano and the drums from a very young age and loved to sing around the house. At the age of 12 he entered a singing competition and got a taste of the limelight, setting him on the road to stardom.

IF JUSTIN COULD DO ANY OTHER JOB IT WOULD BE... AN ARCHITECT! WHO WOULDN'T WANT TO LIVE IN A BIEBER BUILDING!

JUSTIN ONCE WENT BUSKING TO TRY AND RAISE THE MONEY TO GO TO DISNEYLAND. HE GOT THERE IN THE END AND IT'S NOW ONE OF HIS FAVE PLACES IN THE WORLD!

Turn to page 20 to discover more about the most important peeps in Justin's childhood – his family!

TALENT SPOTTING

Check out these swoonsome selfies of JB.
Can you spot which two are exactly same?

1

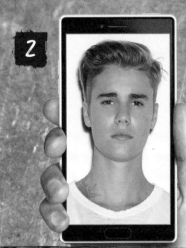
2

3

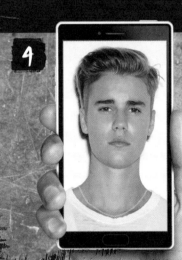
4

5

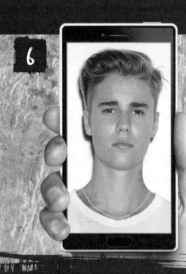
6

7

8

9

Can you spot 5 differences between
these two pics of the boy wonder?

Too easy, now find 10 differences
between these two pics, too.

ANSWERS ON PAGE 60

TOP TRACKS

In December 2015, JB's new album *Purpose* went straight to No 1 all over the world, giving Biebs his sixth No 1 album. With around 500,000 copies sold in its first week, (JB's biggest sales week yet) it was packed with hits!

WHAT DO YOU MEAN?

Bieber's first No 1 was *What Do You Mean?*. It rocketed to the top of the charts all over the world in 2015 and broke the record for most Spotify streams, with 21 million in just 5 days.
Best line: "When you nod your head yes but wanna say no."

SORRY

Sorry also hit the sweet spot of No 1. Produced by Skrillex and Blood Diamonds it bumped Adele off the top spot and was replaced by Biebs' next hit *Love Yourself*.
Best line: "Cos I need just one more chance at second chances."

LOVE YOURSELF

Co written by Ed Sheeran and Bejamin Levin, JB's third No 1 is one of his fave hits from *Purpose*. The acoustic ballad tells the tale of a girl who's used his name to up her own profile and broken his heart.
Best line: "My mamma don't like you and she likes everyone."

NO PRESSURE

Another romantic tune penned to an ex, this top tune is full of remorse but also hope, that one day, his ex will take him back.
Best line: "You ain't gotta make up your mind right now."

LIFE IS WORTH LIVING

A dreamy song of hope and encouragement to all Beliebers that life is worth it. JB asks everyone not to judge others or him. Nobody is perfect and everyone makes mistakes.
Best line: "People make mistakes, doesn't mean you have to give in."

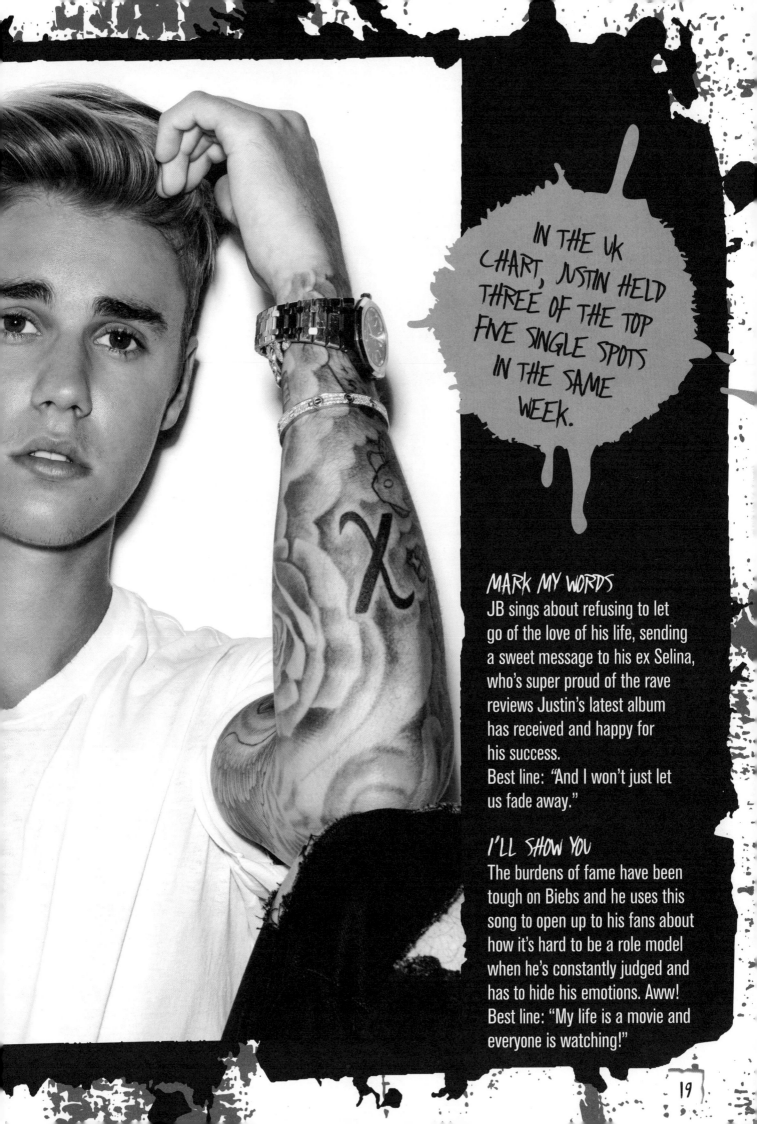

IN THE UK CHART, JUSTIN HELD THREE OF THE TOP FIVE SINGLE SPOTS IN THE SAME WEEK.

MARK MY WORDS

JB sings about refusing to let go of the love of his life, sending a sweet message to his ex Selina, who's super proud of the rave reviews Justin's latest album has received and happy for his success.
Best line: "And I won't just let us fade away."

I'LL SHOW YOU

The burdens of fame have been tough on Biebs and he uses this song to open up to his fans about how it's hard to be a role model when he's constantly judged and has to hide his emotions. Aww!
Best line: "My life is a movie and everyone is watching!"

FAMILY FIRST

Despite his HUGE fame and fortune, home is where JB's heart is and his family are still the most important peeps in his life.

PARENT POWER

Justin's folks were still teenagers when they had him and split up when he was little. While JB didn't have as much as other people when he was growing up, he believes it only made him stronger amd more determined to succeed.

Justin's dad, Jeremy, loves music and got JB into rock from a young age, playing him hits by legendary bands like Guns n Roses.

Justin's mum, Pattie Mallette, has been with him every step on his road to stardom. She admits she made some mistakes when she was younger, but turned her life around when JB was born.

JB's mum is famous in her own right, with millions of Twitter and Instagram followers and her own book *Nowhere But Up*.

 @pattiemallette

BEST BRO EVER

Justin's younger brother and sis, Jazmyn and Jaxon, are treated like VIPs wherever they go. Justin loves getting his siblings up on stage with him, throwing them amazing parties and once took Jazmyn to Disneyland to cheer her up after she broke her arm.

GREAT GRANDIES

When Justin was young, his mum Pattie had to work long hours to make ends meet, so Justin was looked after a lot by his grandparents, Bruce and Diane Dale. JB looks up to them as relationship role models, as they love each other so much. Awwww!

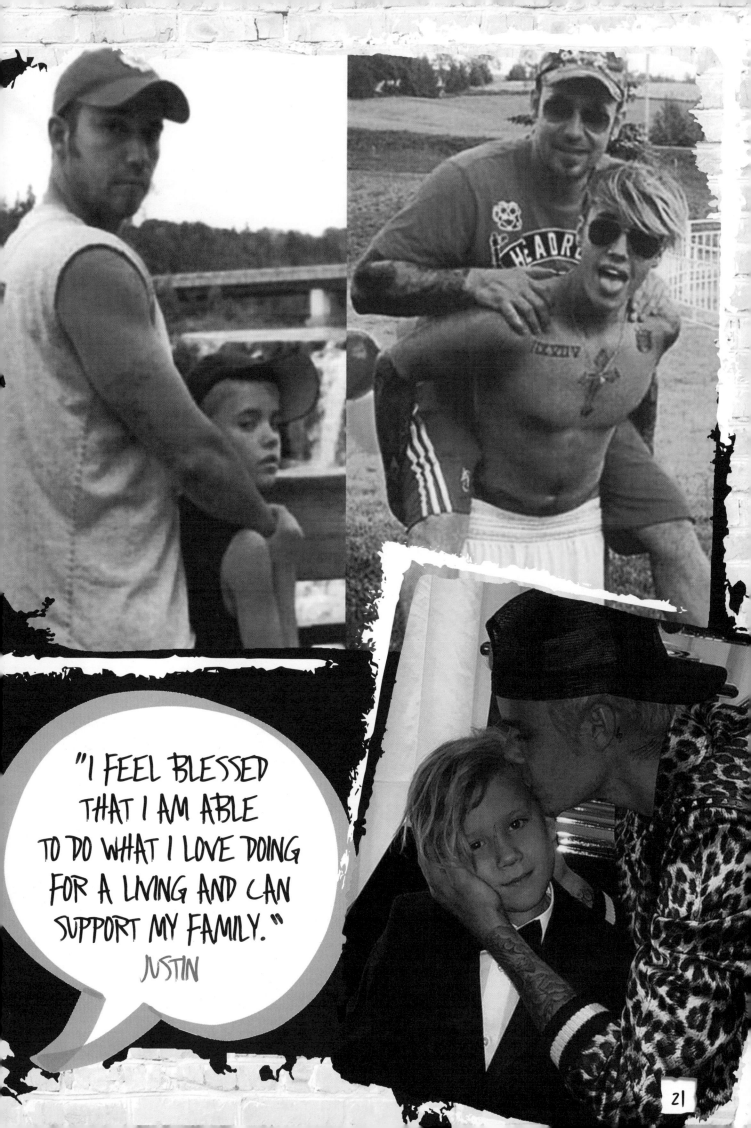

"I FEEL BLESSED THAT I AM ABLE TO DO WHAT I LOVE DOING FOR A LIVING AND CAN SUPPORT MY FAMILY."

JUSTIN

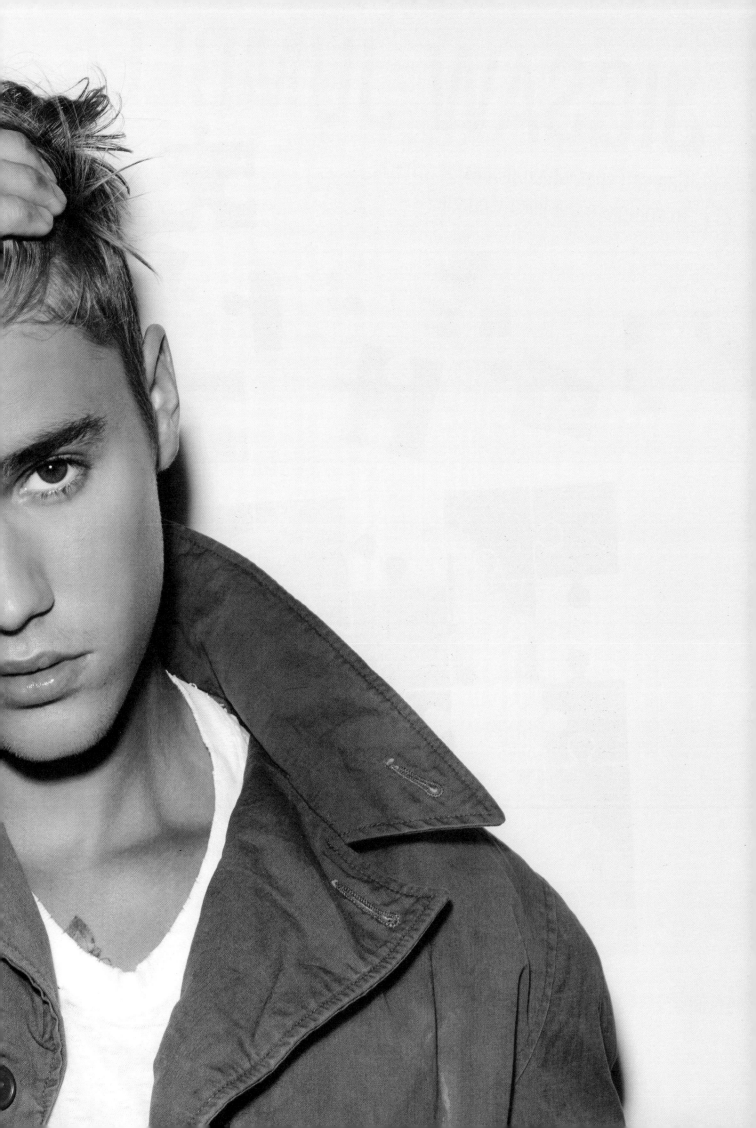

JIGSAW JUMBLE

Can you spot which pieces go where,
to complete the jigsaw puzzle?

#GETCLOSER

Oops! Some of Justin's fans have taken some truly terrible pics of the star. Can you work out what they are of?

A

B

C

D

MUSIC MOOD

Take the test to find out which JB tune you're most in the mood for...

START HERE

Ready to chill or party?

PARTY

CHILL

Need something new or nostalgic?

NEW

NOSTALGIC

DANCE

Love to remember memories or always looking forward?

Want to dance or catch some zzzzzs?

REMEMBER

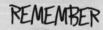

Do you daydream too much?

LOOK FORWARD

SNOOZE

YEP

NOPE

POP

Have you just had a row or great day out with your BFF?

BAD DAY

GOOD DAY

Time for some pop or R&B?

R&B

IN SEQUENCE

Shuffle or sequence listening?

SHUFFLE

Are you feeling glass ½ full or ½ empty?

EMPTY

FULL

Is it hot or cold outside?

COLD

HOT

OUT WITH FRIENDS

HEAR IT

Karaoke queen or lay back and listen?

SING IT

Best place to listen to music?

HOME ALONE

SORRY
Indulge in a bit of 'me time', zone out and tune into JB's soulful *Sorry*! Soothe your senses and let his lyrics work their magic.

BEAUTY AND A BEAT
All true Beliebers can't help bopping along to this little beaut – guaranteed to get your toes tapping, shoulders shaking and lips twitching into a great big smile.

MISTLETOE
Who can resist a Christmas song? Especially one by JB that includes reindeer, snow, and schmoozing under the mistletoe! A perfect present of a tune, wrapped in festive fun.

WHERE ARE U NOW?
Dance like nobody's watching, sing like nobody's listening and lose yourself in the brilliant beats of JB's Grammy award-winning hit.

27

THE PERFORMER

Justin showed raw talent from a young age but he wasn't an overnight success. His road to fame and fortune was a long and hard one, with lots of bumps along the way. But he never gave up!

PRACTISE MAKES PERFECT

In 2007, a 12-year-old Justin entered his first talent comp in his home town of Statford, but failed to win. Never one to give up, Justin took his music to the streets and busked every weekend on the steps of Stratford Theatre, entertaining the locals as they passed him by.

TRUE TALENT

Justin's mum, Pattie, proudly posted vids of a very young JB on YouTube every time he learnt a new song. As the years passed, he gained more and more followers and fans, and the music industry started to take an interest in the cute Canadian with a big voice.

"WHEN I MET HIM, HIS PERSONALITY WON ME OVER. WHEN HE SANG I REALISED WE WERE DEALING WITH THE REAL THING."
USHER

JUSTIN TIMBERLAKE WAS ALSO INTERESTED IN SIGNING JUSTIN, BUT USHER BEAT HIM TO THE DEAL.

DEAL MAKER

Scooter Braun came across Justin's videos on YouTube and, recognizing his talent, contacted Pattie to set up meetings between Justin and some music producers in Atlanta. At first Pattie ignored Scooter's calls, but decided to give him a chance, and was thrilled when Scooter introduced Justin to the talented music coach, Mama Jan and pop sensation, Usher.

BIG BREAK

Usher knew talent when he saw it and saw off stiff competition to offer and secure Justin a record deal. Justin's time had come. He quickly set to work on his first single, *One Time*, and debut album, *My World*.

HIT AFTER HIT

The music poured out of Justin and five further albums quickly followed. *Never Say Never* and *Under the Mistletoe* were released in 2011, both topping the charts in the US and Canada. Next came *Believe* in 2012, *Journals* in 2013 and the best-selling *Purpose* in 2015.

ON TOUR

Beliebers all over the world will get the chance to see their idol in the flesh this year, as JB hits the road for his third worldwide roadtrip, The Purpose World Tour!

SHOWTIME
It's no secret that Justin loves ALL of his fans and this year is determined to see as many of them as he can, by putting on a whopping 64 shows. The tour promises to take fans on a journey, showing how JB hit the big time and his struggle to get there.

TOUR BUDDIES
Justin was joined on his Believe tour by Carly Rae Jepsen, Cody Simpson and Jaden Smith. This year's line up promises to be just as amazing with Postie Malone and Moxie Raia kicking off the show, on the US leg of the tour.

"IT'S BEEN PRETTY AMAZING. I'M GLAD I GET TO TRAVEL THE WORLD AND I'M JUST REALLY THANKFUL THAT I'VE BEEN ABLE TO DO WHAT I LOVE."
JUSTIN

TOUR DATES 2016

MARCH 9 - SEATTLE, WA @ KEYARENA AT SEATTLE CENTER
MARCH 11 - VANCOUVER, BC @ PEPSI LIVE! AT ROGERS ARENA
MARCH 13 - PORTLAND, OR @ MODA CENTER AT THE ROSE QUARTER
MARCH 15 - SACRAMENTO, CA @ SLEEP TRAIN ARENA
MARCH 17 - SAN JOSE, CA @ SAP CENTER AT SAN JOSE
MARCH 18 - OAKLAND, CA @ ORACLE ARENA
MARCH 20 - LOS ANGELES, CA @ STAPLES CENTER
MARCH 21 - LOS ANGELES, CA @ STAPLES CENTER
MARCH 25 - LAS VEGAS, NV @ MGM GRAND GARDEN ARENA
MARCH 26 - FRESNO, CA @ SAVE MART CENTER
MARCH 29 - SAN DIEGO, CA @ VALLEY VIEW CASINO CENTER
MARCH 30 - GLENDALE, AZ @ GILA RIVER ARENA
APRIL 2 - SALT LAKE CITY, UT @ VIVINT SMART HOME ARENA
APRIL 4 - DENVER, CO @ PEPSI CENTER
APRIL 6 - KANSAS CITY, MO @ SPRINT CENTER
APRIL 7 - TULSA, OK @ BOK CENTER
APRIL 9 - HOUSTON, TX @ TOYOTA CENTER
APRIL 10 - DALLAS, TX @ AMERICAN AIRLINES CENTER
APRIL 12 - ATLANTA, GA @ PHILIPS ARENA
APRIL 19 - ST. LOUIS, MO @ SCOTTRADE CENTER
APRIL 20 - LOUISVILLE, KY @ KFC YUM! CENTER
APRIL 22 - ROSEMONT, IL @ ALLSTATE ARENA
APRIL 23 - ROSEMONT, IL @ ALLSTATE ARENA
APRIL 25 - AUBURN HILLS, MI @ THE PALACE OF AUB URN HILLS
APRIL 26 - CLEVELAND, OH @ QUICKEN LOANS ARENA
APRIL 28 - COLUMBUS, OH @ SCHOTTENSTEIN CENTER
APRIL 29 - WASHINGTON, DC @ VERIZON CENTER
MAY 4 - BROOKLYN, NY @ BARCLAYS CENTER
MAY 5 - BROOKLYN, NY @ BARCLAYS CENTER
MAY 7 - PHILADELPHIA, PA @ WELLS FARGO CENTER
MAY 10 - BOSTON, MA @ TD GARDEN
MAY 13 - OTTAWA, ON @ CANADIAN TIRE CENTRE
MAY 14 - QUEBEC CITY, BC @ VIDEOTRON CENTRE
MAY 16 - MONTREAL, BC @ BELL CENTRE
MAY 18 - TORONTO, ON @ AIR CANADA CENTRE
MAY 19 - TORONTO, ON @ AIR CANADA CENTRE

JUNE 11 - WINNIPEG, MB @ MTS CENTRE
JUNE 13 - CALGARY, AB @ SCOTIABANK SADDLEDOME
JUNE 14 - EDMONTON, AB @ REXALL PLACE
JUNE 16 - SASKATOON, SK @ CREDIT UNION CENTRE
JUNE 18 - FARGO, ND @ FARGODOME
JUNE 19 - MINNEAPOLIS, MN @ TARGET CENTER
JUNE 21 - LINCOLN, NE @ PINNACLE BANK ARENA
JUNE 22 - DES MOINES, IA @ WELLS FARGO ARENA
JUNE 24 - CINCINNATI, OH @ U.S. BANK ARENA
JUNE 25 - INDIANAPOLIS, IN @ BANKERS LIFE FIELDHOUSE
JUNE 27 - NASHVILLE, TN @ BRIDGESTONE ARENA
JUNE 29 - JACKSONVILLE, FL @ JACKSONVILLE VETS MEMORIAL ARENA
JUNE 30 - ORLANDO, FL @ AMWAY CENTER
JULY 2 - MIAMI, FL @ AMERICANAIRLINES ARENA
JULY 6 - GREENSBORO, NC @ GREENSBORO COLISEUM
JULY 7 - BALTIMORE, MD @ ROYAL FARMS ARENA
JULY 9 - NEWARK, NJ @ PRUDENTIAL CENTER
JULY 10 - HARTFORD, CT @ XL CENTER
JULY 12 - BUFFALO, NY @ FIRST NIAGARA CENTER
JULY 13 - PITTSBURGH, PA @ CONSOL ENERGY CENTER
JULY 15 - ATLANTIC CITY, NJ @ BOARDWALK HALL
JULY 18 - NEW YORK CITY, NY @ MADISON SQUARE GARDEN
JULY 19 - NEW YORK CITY, NY @ MADISON SQUARE GARDEN
SEPTEMBER 8 - KOPAVOGUR, ICELAND @ KORINN
SEPTEMBER 9 - KOPAVOGUR, ICELAND @ KORINN
SEPTEMBER 14 – BERLIN, GERMANY @ MERCEDES-BENZ ARENA
SEPTEMBER 16 – MUNICH, GERMANY @ OLYMPIAHALLE
SEPTEMBER 18 – COLOGNE, GERMANY @ LANXESS ARENA
SEPTEMBER 20 – PARIS, FRANCE @ ACCORHOTELS ARENA
SEPTEMBER 23 – OSLO, NORWAY @ TELENOR ARENA
SEPTEMBER 26 – HELSINKI, FINLAND @ HARTWALL ARENA
SEPTEMBER 29 - STOCKHOLM, SWEDEN @ TELE2 ARENA
OCTOBER 2 – COPENHAGEN, DENMARK @ TELIA PARKEN
OCTOBER 5 – ANTWERP, BELGIUM @ SPORTSPALAIS
OCTOBER 6 – ANTWERP, BELGIUM @ SPORTSPALAIS
OCTOBER 8 – ARNHEM, NETHERLANDS @ GELREDOME
OCTOBER 11 – LONDON, ENGLAND @ THE O2
OCTOBER 12 – LONDON, ENGLAND @ THE O2
OCTOBER 17 – BIRMINGHAM, ENGLAND @ BARCLAYCARD ARENA
OCTOBER 18 – BIRMINGHAM, ENGLAND @ BARCLAYCARD ARENA
OCTOBER 20 – MANCHESTER, ENGLAND @ MANCHESTER ARENA
OCTOBER 21 – MANCHESTER, ENGLAND @ MANCHESTER ARENA
OCTOBER 26 – SHEFFIELD, ENGLAND @ SHEFFIELD ARENA
OCTOBER 27 – GLASGOW, SCOTLAND @ SSE HYDRO
NOVEMBER 1 – DUBLIN, IRELAND @ 3ARENA
NOVEMBER 8 – VIENNA, AUSTRIA @ WIENER STADTHALLE
NOVEMBER 11 – KRAKÓW, POLAND @ TAURON ARENA
NOVEMBER 12 – PRAGUE, CZECH REPUBLIC @ O2 ARENA
NOVEMBER 14 – HAMBURG, GERMANY @ BARCLAYCARD ARENA
NOVEMBER 16 – FRANKFURT, GERMANY @ FESTHALLE
NOVEMBER 17 – ZURICH, SWITZERLAND @ HALLENSTADION
NOVEMBER 19 – BOLOGNA, ITALY @ UNIPOL ARENA
NOVEMBER 20 – BOLOGNA, ITALY @ UNIPOL ARENA
NOVEMBER 22 – BARCELONA, SPAIN @ PALAU SANT JORDI
NOVEMBER 23 – MADRID, SPAIN @ BARCLAYCARD CENTER
NOVEMBER 25 – LISBON, PORTUGAL @ MEO ARENA

EMOTICON SUDOKU

Practise doodling these emoticons in the space below, then draw them into the grids to complete the puzzles. There can only be one of each emoticon in each column, row and two-by-two square.

ANSWERS ON PAGE 60

STYLE ICON

Not content with cracking the music industry, JB is fast becoming a fashionista favourite too... he even has his own line of t-shirts out!

STEAL HIS STYLE

BIEBS LOVES HIS BLING!

JB loves...

SUNGLASSES

BEANIES

CAPS

BLING

VESTS

TRAINERS

JB'S HAIR IS CONSTANTLY CHANGING. KEEP UP!

COOL SHADES ARE A MUST, EVEN IN WINTER.

SLOUCHY, SOFT KNITS HELP ROCK THE LOOK.

JUSTIN'S GO-TO FASHION FAVE IS A COOL AND COMFY PAIR OF JEANS.

Time for tees

Help Justin out with his latest
t-shirt designs and create some
of your own designs below.

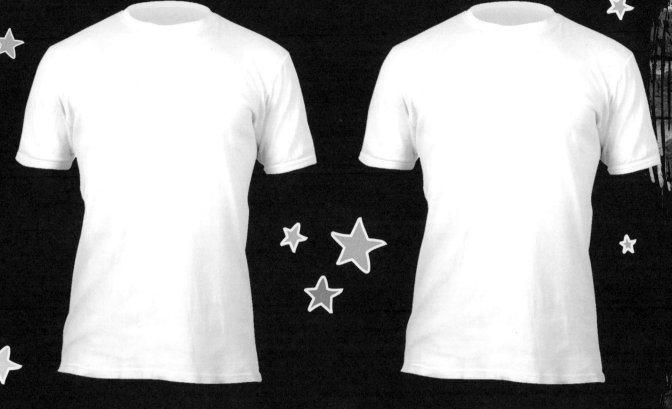

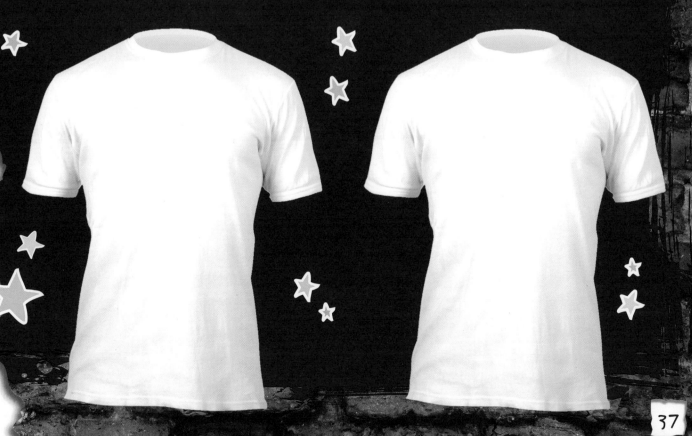

BIEBER BABBLE

Test your true fan status by matching the words to the right meanings to see how well you speak Belieber!

1

What would Bieber do? (Question to ask oneself when faced with a tough decision.)

BIEBER FEVER

2

Obsessive Justin Bieber Disorder.

BIEBER BLAST

3

To give a touch of Bieber to a person or object.

BIEBER BULLIED

5

Name of a true fan.

4

To conspire with other fans to download a Bieber release, to ensure its success.

TEAM BIEBER

EAGER BIEBER

6

Part of the inner core and only something a true fan can claim to be part of.

ANSWERS ON PAGE 60

BELIEBER

OMB

7

An obsessive fan of JB.

OJBD

8

Term favourited
by JB to describe
a good-looking girl.

BIEBERGASTED

9

Exclamation often used
to express shock/awe.

10

To be given a hard time
about loving JB.

NON-BELIEBER

SHAWTY

11

Not a JB fan.

12

Word used to describe someone
overwhelmed by their love of JB.

BIEBERSTRUCK

13

To be shocked by the wonder
of all things Justin Bieber.

WWBD?

14

The physical effect
JB has on his fans.

BIEBERFIED

MUSIC MASTER

We all love a good Bieber beat, but it's only when you really listen to JB's lyrics that you realize how truly magical his music is. But what are the magic ingredients?

INSPIRED LYRICS

During an interview with Ellen DeGeneres, Biebs admitted that three of his songs from *Purpose* were about his ex, Selina Gomez, Sorry, *What Do You Mean?* and *Mark My Words.* Other tracks for this and past albums are inspired by his friends, family and of course, you, his amazing fans.

"I WROTE BELIEVE FOR MY FANS AND HOW THEY INSPIRED ME. IT MEANS A LOT."
JUSTIN

COLLABS

From Drake, Will.i.am and Nicki Minaj to Big Sean, Skrillex, Ed Sheeran and Jack Ü, nobody does a better music collab than JB. His knack of picking the perfect partner for his tunes shows his growth as an artist, as he effortlessly blends hip-hop, rap and R&B with his smooth vocals. Quite simply, he rocks.

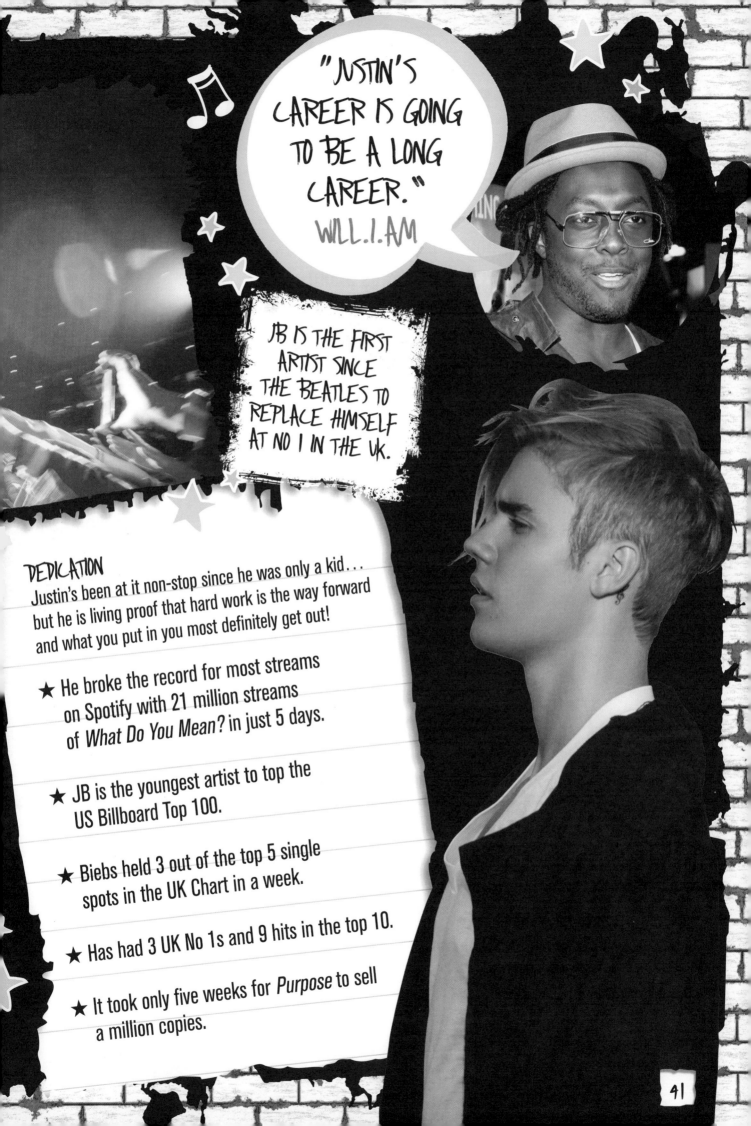

"JUSTIN'S CAREER IS GOING TO BE A LONG CAREER."
WILL.I.AM

JB IS THE FIRST ARTIST SINCE THE BEATLES TO REPLACE HIMSELF AT NO 1 IN THE UK.

DEDICATION

Justin's been at it non-stop since he was only a kid... but he is living proof that hard work is the way forward and what you put in you most definitely get out!

★ He broke the record for most streams on Spotify with 21 million streams of *What Do You Mean?* in just 5 days.

★ JB is the youngest artist to top the US Billboard Top 100.

★ Biebs held 3 out of the top 5 single spots in the UK Chart in a week.

★ Has had 3 UK No 1s and 9 hits in the top 10.

★ It took only five weeks for *Purpose* to sell a million copies.

PEN PERSONALITY

According to handwriting experts, signatures can reveal a lot about a person. Take a look at JB's below and what it tells us about the boy wonder himself...

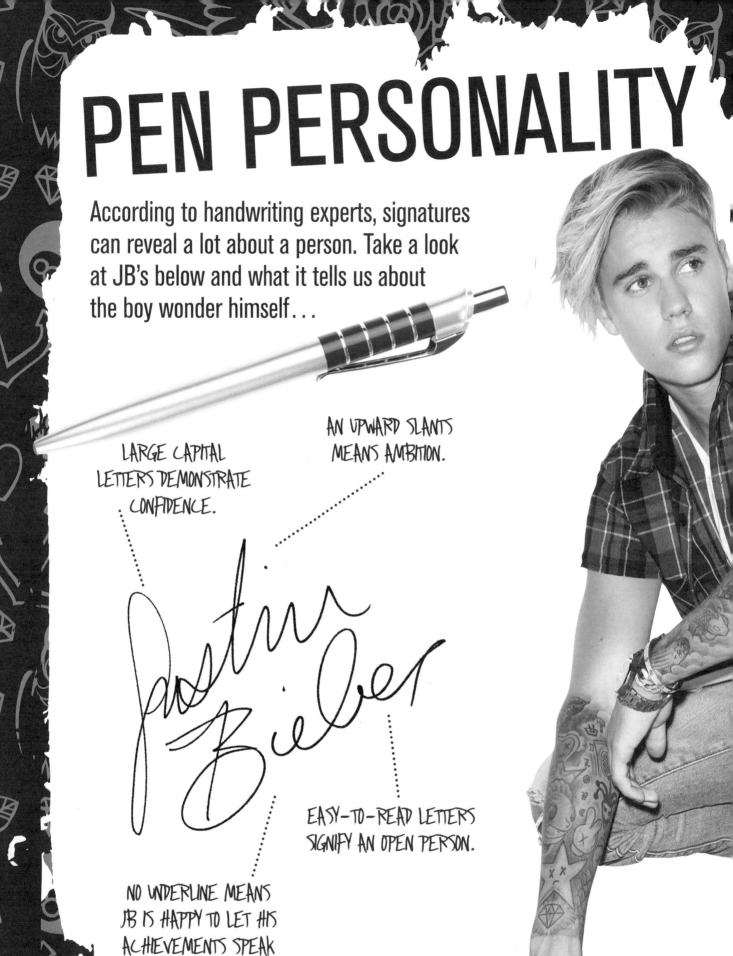

LARGE CAPITAL LETTERS DEMONSTRATE CONFIDENCE.

AN UPWARD SLANTS MEANS AMBITION.

EASY-TO-READ LETTERS SIGNIFY AN OPEN PERSON.

NO UNDERLINE MEANS JB IS HAPPY TO LET HIS ACHIEVEMENTS SPEAK FOR THEMSELVES.

Now practise your own signature in the space below and read on to discover what it says about you.

Jody Marleen

Easy-to-read letters - an open personality
Hard-to-read letters - a private personality
Easy-to-read first name but hard-to-read last name - places importance on personal accomplishments
No underline - prefers to let personal achievements speak for themselves
Underline - sense of self importance
Closing flick or line at end - drive and determination
Upward slope - sense of ambition, a tendency to look towards the future
Downward slope - pessimistic and cautious
Rising up only towards the end - sense of optimism
No slant - balanced
Nickname - independent and confident in own abilities
Initials only - a very private person
No dot on 'i' - reluctant to dwell on small details, a bigger-picture person
Pronounced capital letters - confident, a strong sense of self-worth
No surname - relaxed approach to life
Scribbled - sharp intelligence and busy lifestyle
Large first letter - strives to make presence felt

DOWNTIME

He doesn't have a lot of it, but when JB manages to steal a bit of time for himself, read on to discover what he likes to do with it.

SK8R BOI

Even when he's working, like during a recent *GQ* fashion shoot, JB loves to cruise around on his skateboard. He can do some nifty tricks and loves nothing more than skating with famous pals, like Lil' Wayne.

ICE COOL

Sports mad from a young age, JB loves ice hockey and hits the ice whenever he can. His fave team is the Toronto Maple Leafs, from his native Canada.

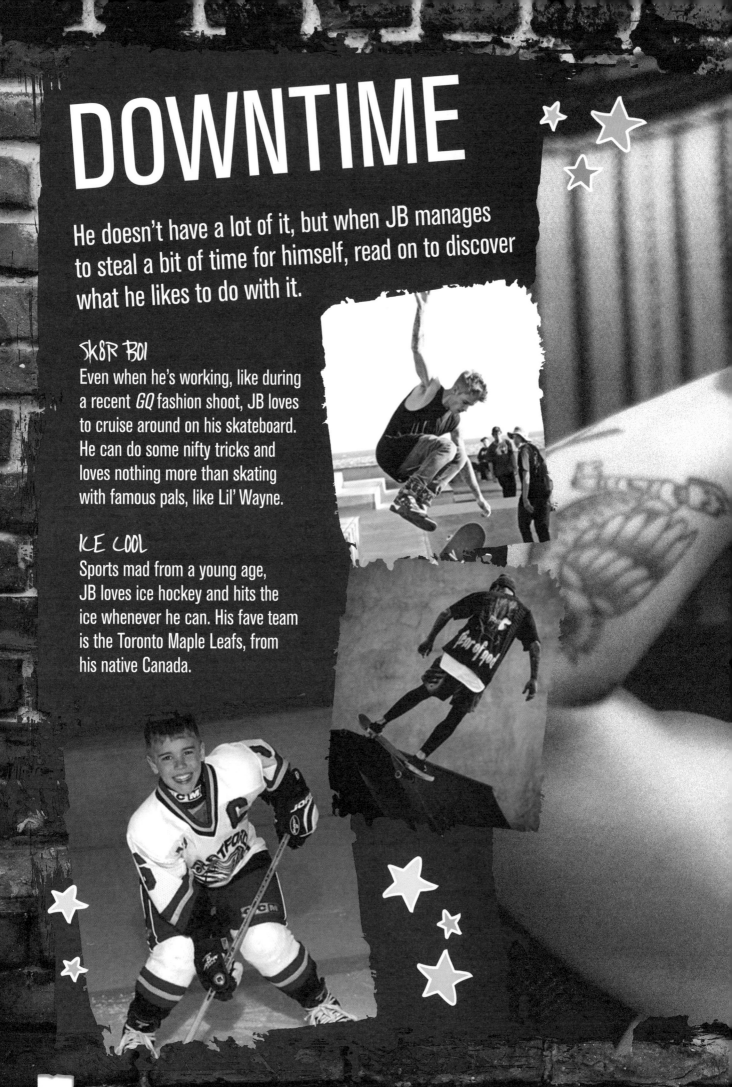

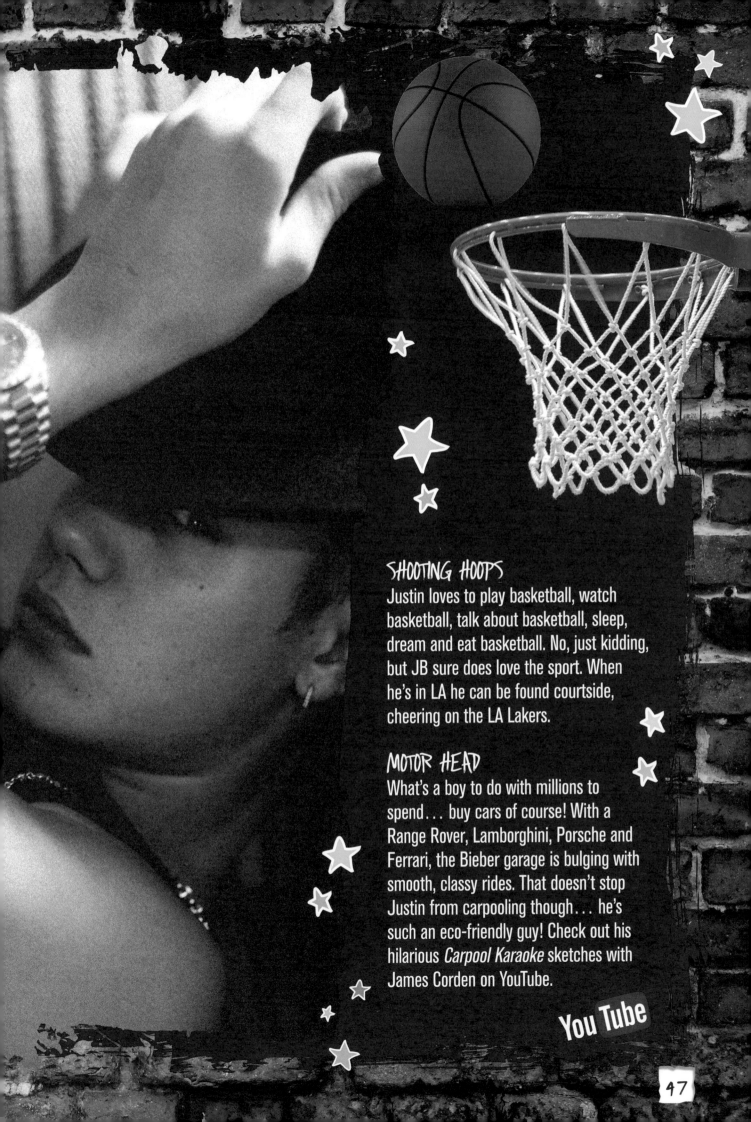

SHOOTING HOOPS

Justin loves to play basketball, watch basketball, talk about basketball, sleep, dream and eat basketball. No, just kidding, but JB sure does love the sport. When he's in LA he can be found courtside, cheering on the LA Lakers.

MOTOR HEAD

What's a boy to do with millions to spend... buy cars of course! With a Range Rover, Lamborghini, Porsche and Ferrari, the Bieber garage is bulging with smooth, classy rides. That doesn't stop Justin from carpooling though... he's such an eco-friendly guy! Check out his hilarious *Carpool Karaoke* sketches with James Corden on YouTube.

You Tube

OODLES OF DOODLES

TURN THESE SQUIGGLES INTO SOMETHING ELSE.

WHAT DO YOU THINK JUSTIN IS DREAMING OF?

ME

CRANK UP YOUR FAVOURITE JB TUNE, CLOSE YOUR EYES, LISTEN, THEN DOODLE WHATEVER COMES INTO YOUR HEAD.

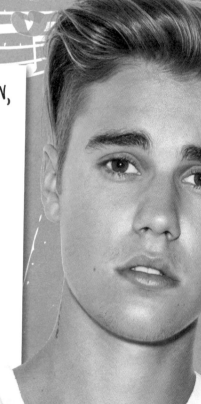

#DOODLE YOURSELF INTO THIS SELFIE WITH JUSTIN. CUTE COUPLE ALERT!

DOODLE SOME COOL ACCESSORIES FOR JB TO WEAR.

TURN THE LETTERS IN JUSTIN'S NAME INTO SOMETHING ELSE WONDERFUL...

JUSTIN

BIEBER

BELIEVE

Justin didn't just dream, he dreamt BIG. He found his purpose and wants his fans to dream big and believe too! What do you dream about?

DREAM JOB:

DREAM CRUSH:

DREAM OUTFIT:

DREAM HOLIDAY:

DREAM HOME:

IF YOU COULD BE ANY OF THE BELOW FOR THE DAY, WHAT WOULD YOU BE...

- [ ] invisible
- [ ] Prime Minister
- [ ] the Queen
- [ ] a pop star
- [ ] Justin Bieber's assistant
- [ ] a millionaire
- [ ] a superhero

"I BELIEVE IN MYSELF, MY DREAMS, THAT I CAN DO ANYTHING."
JUSTIN

USE THE SPACE BELOW TO WRITE DOWN YOUR NIGHT DREAMS, THEN USE THE DREAM DECODER TO WORK OUT WHAT THEY MIGHT MEAN.

DAY:
WHAT HAPPENS:

WHAT DOES IT MEAN:

DAY:
WHAT HAPPENS:

WHAT DOES IT MEAN:

DAY:
WHAT HAPPENS:

WHAT DOES IT MEAN:

DREAM DECODER

FALLING DREAMS

If you dream you are falling, from the sky, down a hole or off a cliff, it can mean that you feel out of control. Try to work out what area of your life you need to take control of, and what you can do about it, and these dreams will stop.

FLYING DREAMS

If you dream you are flying, it means you feel confident and secure about your life and in control. If you dream you are flying too high, it can mean you are concerned how your success might change your life.

BEING NAKED DREAMS

Ever dream you've forgotten to put your clothes on? It usually means you're feeling a bit worried about something. It can also mean you are trying to hide your true self.

SONG SELFIE

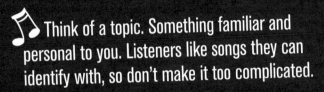

Channel your inner Justin and create your own musical poetry with a pop song about your life!

♫ Think of a topic. Something familiar and personal to you. Listeners like songs they can identify with, so don't make it too complicated.

♫ Be as honest as you can be when writing your thoughts and feelings. That way they'll really connect with your listeners.

♫ Follow a simple structure like verse 1, chorus, verse 2, chorus, verse 3, chorus, bridge, chorus.

♫ When creating your rhymes, follow patterns like ABAB or AABB.

♫ Good luck!

A LITTLE HELPING HAND...
USE THIS SPACE TO THINK OF SOME THEMES
FOR YOUR SONG.

DREAMS

HOPES

LOVE

USE THIS SPACE TO THINK OF SOME
EASY RHYMING WORDS.

YOU

TOO

TRUE

BLUE

DO

MY SONG

WHO WOULD YOUR SONG BE ABOUT?

MY FAVE JB LYRICS ARE...
_____
_____
_____
_____

CHANGE JUSTIN'S LYRICS TO SOMETHING TOTALLY DIFFERENT...
IS IT TOO LATE TO SAY I'M...
_____
_____
_____
_____
_____

A TO Z OF JUSTIN BIEBER

A is for abs! Mmmmmm!

B is for Beliebers of course. Who else?

C is for Christmas... who doesn't love his festive *Under the Mistletoe* album.

D is for dancer. The boy sure can move.

E is for his collab with Sean Kingston, *Eenie Meenie*.

F is for fun, something which JB knows how to have a lot of!

G is for a Grammy. Yessssss! JB finally got one in 2016.

H is for help. Justin does his bit for loads of different charities, to help out those less fortunate than he is.

I is for internet. Justin is one of the most-Googled stars on the planet.

J is for Jaxon and Jasmyn. The cutest siblings a big bro could ever ask for.

K is for karaoke, something JB does best, in a car, with James Corden.

L is for left-handed. Yep, Justin's a leftie.

M is for *My World*, JB's first studio album.

N is for *Never Say Never*, Justin's hugely successful 3D concert film.

O is for OMB. Forget OMG, with true Beliebers, it's gotta be OH MY BIEBER!

P is for Pattie. If it wasn't for her, Justin may never have achieved all he has.

Q is for questions, which JB tries to answer as many as he can from his fans.

R is for remix and boy does Bieber do them well.

S is for Scooter, Justin's manager, who discovered him on YouTube and led him to stardom.

T is for Twitter, 80 million followers and growing by the minute.

U is for Usher, who played a key part in launching Justin's career and is still a close friend.

V is for voice. And what a voice it is!

W is for world domination. And if there are aliens out there, we're sure Justin would be massive on Mars too!

X is for x-tra special!

Y is for YouTube, where it all began.

You Tube

Z is for zodiac. Justin is a true Pisces, devoted and imaginative.

QUIZ

Put your Belieber know-how to the test with our bumper Bieber quiz!

1 AT WHAT AGE DID JUSTIN START POSTING HIS SONGS ON YOU TUBE?

☐ 8 ☐ 12 ☐ 16

2 WHICH OF THESE IS JB'S FAVE FOOD?

☐ spag bol

☐ burger

☐ nachos

3 WHAT ARE THE NAMES OF JUSTIN'S PARENTS?

☐ Jeremy and Pattie

☐ John and Pam

☐ Jerry and Penny

4 WHICH SPORT IS JUSTIN A HUGE FAN OF?

☐ sailing

☐ archery

☐ ice hockey

5 WHICH FAMOUS POP STAR HELPED LAUNCH JUSTIN'S CAREER?

☐ Adam Levine

☐ Ed Sheeran

☐ Usher

6 WHICH OF THESE IS NOT A JUSTIN BIEBER SONG?

☐ *Somebody to Love*

☐ *Love Yourself*

☐ *Love Hurts*

7 WHICH OF THESE POP LADEEZ HAS JB COLABBED WITH?

- ☐ Madonna
- ☐ Nicky Minaj
- ☐ Taylor Swift

8 WHEN JUSTIN WRITES HIS AMAZING SONGS, WHICH HAND DOES HE WRITE WITH?

- ☐ left
- ☐ right
- ☐ both

9 WHOSE EYE HAS BIEBS GOT TATTOOED ON HIS ARM?

- ☐ Scooter Braun's
- ☐ his mum, Pattie's
- ☐ Ellen DeGeneres'

ANSWERS ON PAGE 60

ANSWERS

p8-9

LOVE YOURSELF
And tried to make me forget where I came from
SORRY
Can we both say the words and forget this
NEVER LET YOU GO
If you don't know, this is love
BABY
She woke me up daily, don't need no Starbucks

p12-13

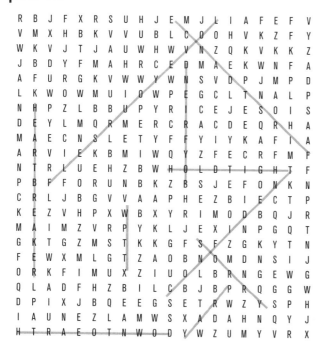

p16 3 and 7 are the same

p17

p24

1-C, 2-J, 3-G, 4-B, 5-D, 6-F, 7-A, 8-H, 9-K, 10-E

p25

A=star tattoo on arm, B=knee with ripped jeans
C=wrist with watch, D=hair

p32

p56-57

1=WWBD, 2=OJBD, 3=Bieberfied, 4=Bieber
Blast, 5=Belieber, 6=Team Bieber, 7=Eager
Bieber, 8=Shawty, 9=OMB, 10=Bieber
Bullied, 11=Non Belieber, 12=Bieberstruck,
13=Biebergasted, 14=Bieber Fever

p56

1 = 12
2 = spag bol
3 = Jeremy and Pattie
4 = ice hockey
5 = Usher
6 = *Somebody to Love*
7 = Madonna
8 = left
9 = his mum, Pattie's